FEAR &

ANXIETY

Learning to Overcome with God's Truth

LOVEGODGREATLY.COM

**AT LOVE GOD GREATLY, YOU'LL FIND
REAL, AUTHENTIC WOMEN. WOMEN WHO
ARE IMPERFECT, YET FORGIVEN.**

Women who desire less of us, and a whole lot
more of Jesus. Women who long to know God
through His Word, because we know that Truth
transforms and sets us free. Women who are
better together, saturated in God's Word and in
community with one another.

Welcome, friend. We're so glad you're here...

CONTENTS

WELCOME

We are glad you have decided to join us in this Bible study! First of all, please know that you have been prayed for! It is not a coincidence you are participating in this study.

Our prayer for you is simple: that you will grow closer to our Lord as you dig into His Word each and every day! As you develop the discipline of being in God's Word on a daily basis, our prayer is that you will fall in love with Him even more as you spend time reading from the Bible.

Each day before you read the assigned Scripture(s), pray and ask God to help you understand it. Invite Him to speak to you through His Word. Then listen. It's His job to speak to you, and it's your job to listen and obey.

Take time to read the verses over and over again. We are told in Proverbs to search and you will find: "Search for it like silver, and hunt for it like hidden treasure. Then you will understand" (Prov. 2:4–5 NCV).

All of us here at Love God Greatly can't wait for you to get started, and we hope to see you at the finish line. Endure, persevere, press on—and don't give up! Finish well what you are beginning today. We will be here every step of the way, cheering you on! We are in this together. Fight to rise early, to push back the stress of the day, to sit alone and spend time in God's Word! Let's see what God has in store for you in this study! Journey with us as we learn to love God greatly with our lives!

As you go through this study, join us in the following resources below:

Weekly Blog Posts •

Weekly Memory Verses •

Weekly Challenges •

Facebook, Twitter, Instagram •

LoveGodGreatly.com •

Hashtags: #LoveGodGreatly •

RESOURCES

Join Us

ONLINE
lovegodgreatly.com

STORE
lovegodgreatly.com/store

FACEBOOK
facebook.com/LoveGodGreatly

INSTAGRAM
instagram.com/lovegodgreatlyofficial

TWITTER
@_LoveGodGreatly

DOWNLOAD THE APP

CONTACT US
info@lovegodgreatly.com

CONNECT
#LoveGodGreatly

LOVE
GOD
GREATLY

Love God Greatly (LGG) is a beautiful community of women who use a variety of technology platforms to keep each other accountable in God's Word. We start with a simple Bible reading plan, but it doesn't stop there.

Some women gather in homes and churches locally, while others connect online with women across the globe. Whatever the method, we lovingly lock arms and unite for this purpose: to love God greatly with our lives.

Would you consider reaching out and doing this study with someone?

In today's fast-paced technology-driven world, it would be easy to study God's Word in an isolated environment that lacks encouragement or support, but that isn't the intention here at Love God Greatly. God created us to live in community with Him and with those around us.

We need each other, and we live life better together. Because of this, would you consider reaching out and doing this study with someone?

Rest assured we'll be studying right alongside you—learning with you, cheering for you, enjoying sweet fellowship, and smiling from ear to ear as we watch God unite women together—intentionally connecting hearts and minds for His glory.

So here's the challenge: call your mom, your sister, your grandma, the girl across the street, or the college friend across the country. Gather a group of girls from your church or workplace, or meet in a coffee shop with friends you have always wished you knew better.

Arm-in-arm and hand-in-hand, let's do this thing…together.

SOAP STUDY

HOW AND WHY TO SOAP

In this study we offer you a study journal to accompany the verses we are reading. This journal is designed to help you interact with God's Word and learn to dig deeper, encouraging you to slow down and reflect on what God is saying to you that day.

At Love God Greatly, we use the SOAP Bible study method. Before beginning, let's take a moment to define this method and share why we recommend using it during your quiet time in the following pages.

The most important ingredients in the Soap method are your interaction with God's Word and your application of His Word to your life.

It's one thing to simply read Scripture. But when you interact with it, intentionally slowing down to really reflect on it, suddenly words start popping off the page. The SOAP method allows you to dig deeper into Scripture and see more than you would if you simply read the verses and then went on your merry way.

The most important ingredients in the SOAP method are your interaction with God's Word and your application of His Word to your life:

Blessed is the one who does not walk in step with the wicked or stand in the way that sinners take or sit in the company of mockers, but whose delight is in the law of the LORD, and who meditates on his law day and night. That person is like a tree planted by streams of water, which yields its fruit in season and whose leaf does not wither—whatever they do prospers.
(Ps. 1:1–3, NIV)

Please take the time to SOAP through our Bible studies and see for yourself how much more you get from your daily reading.

You'll be amazed.

SOAP STUDY *(CONTINUED)*

WHAT DOES SOAP MEAN?

S STANDS FOR
SCRIPTURE

Physically write out the verses.

You'll be amazed at what God will reveal to you just by taking the time to slow down and write out what you are reading!

O STANDS FOR
OBSERVATION

What do you see in the verses that you're reading?

Who is the intended audience? Is there a repetition of words?

What words stand out to you?

MONDAY

READ
Colossians 1:5–8

SOAP
Colossians 1:5–8

Scripture

WRITE OUT THE SCRIPTURE PASSAGE FOR THE DAY.

The faith and love that spring from the hope stored up for you in heaven and about which you have already heard in the true message of the gospel that has come to you. In the same way, the gospel is bearing fruit and growing throughout the whole world just as it has been doing among you since the day you heard it and truly understood God's grace. You learned it from Epaphras, our dear fellow servant, who is a faithful minister of Christ on our behalf, and who also told us of your love in the Spirit.

Observations

WRITE DOWN 1 OR 2 OBSERVATIONS FROM THE PASSAGE.

When you combine faith and love, you get hope. We must remember that our hope is in heaven; it is yet to come. The gospel is the Word of truth. The gospel is continually bearing fruit and growing from the first day to the last. It just takes one person to change a whole community. Epaphras

A STANDS FOR
APPLICATION

*This is when God's
Word becomes
personal.*

*What is God
saying to you today?*

*How can you apply
what you just read
to your own personal
life?*

*What changes do you
need to make? Is there
action you need to
take?*

Applications

WRITE
DOWN 1 OR 2
APPLICATIONS
FROM THE
PASSAGE.

God used one man, Epaphras, to change a whole town. I was reminded that we are simply called to tell others about Christ it is God's job to spread the gospel, to grow it, and have it bear fruit. I felt today's verses were almost directly spoken to Love God Greatly women: The gospel is bearing fruit and growing throughout the whole world just as it has been doing among you since the day you heard it and truly understood God's grace.

Pray

WRITE OUT
A PRAYER
OVER WHAT
YOU LEARNED
FROM TODAY'S
PASSAGE.

Dear Lord, please help me to be an Epaphras, to tell others about You and then leave the results in Your loving hands. Please help me to understand and apply personally what I have read today to my life, thereby becoming more and more like You each and every day. Help me to live a life that bears the fruit of faith and love, anchoring my hope in heaven, not here on earth. Help me to remember that the best is yet to come!

P STANDS FOR **PRAYER**

Pray God's Word back to Him. Spend time thanking Him.

*If He has revealed something to you during this time in His Word, pray
about it.*

*If He has revealed some sin that is in your life, confess. And remember, He
loves you dearly.*

A RECIPE FOR YOU

RENDANG DAGING SAPI (BEEF IN SPICY COCONUT MILK)

Ingredients

1 1/4 liters coconut milk from 2 old coconuts (or 5 cups of coconut milk, canned works well)

1 turmeric leaf, torn and knotted

5 kaffir lime leaves

1 stalk lemon grass, bruised

1-2 piece of asam gelugur* (can be substitute with dried tamarind skin)

10 red chilies, finely sliced

1 kg beef, fat, and sinew removed, cut into 3 cm cubes (or 2 lbs beef chuck roast)

Spices (ground):

3 tablespoons chopped galangal

1/2 tablespoon chopped turmeric

1/2 tablespoon chopped ginger

200 grams red chilies

4 shallots

salt to season

Directions

- Simmer coconut milk with turmeric leaf, kaffir lime leaves, lemon grass, asam gelugur, sliced chilies and ground spices until the milk thickens and becomes oily.

- Reduce the heat.

- Add beef and cook until tender.

- Stir occasionally until the spices dry and turn brown.

Optional steps:

- Combine rendang with 300 grams small potatoes.

- Soak potatoes in water for 15 minutes then scrub with a soft brush to lean the skin.

- Add to the gravy together with beef.

- Rendang can be kept for a long time in the refrigerator. Heat before serving.

*Also known as Gracinia Atnoviridis. The fruit, which is round, like a tangerine, is usually sliced thinly and dried in the sun. Light brown when fresh, it gradually turns darker as it ages. It has and aromatic flavor and does not discolor the sauce or gravy. In some places it is called dried tamarind skin.

LGG INDONESIAN TESTIMONY

HELEN, UNITED STATES

God opened our eyes to see the need for the Gospel in the languages that the people understand.

My husband and I have been doing short mission trips to Indonesia since 2006, before we got married. And God continues to work and send us to Indonesia to serve along with the nationals to reach people with the Gospel. Indonesia has about 600 more people group languages. Some people who are able to go to school have the opportunity to learn Indonesian as the National Language. Through these mission trips, God opened our eyes to see the need for the Gospel in the languages that the people understand, and also the needs of resources to help believers grow in their faith.

Last year, I discovered Love God Greatly and I was so blessed by the studies I did. I thought "This is it! This study can help Indonesian women to dig deeper and learn more about God's Word. This study can help them to grow in their faith!" There are not many Bible studies like these for women available in the Indonesian language. I contacted Angela and asked if I could translate the study into Indonesian, and she said "Yes!" I am so thankful for the team that has been working to translate the study books for this year. We have 10 books now available in Indonesian!

On our Summer 2017 Mission Trip, I brought some of the Indonesian "You're Forgiven" books with me, which were donated by generous people from the States. God led me to meet and share with some college women cell group leaders, pastor's wives, and missionaries. I gave them the books and they asked if I had more than just one. I told them for now the study guides were available online for them to download, print and make copies. They were so very thankful that the Love God Greatly Bible Studies were available in Indonesian AND available for free to download. They really need resources for Bible study and discipleship.

I praised God for the joy I saw on their faces when they had the books in their hands. There are not many Christian bookstores in Indonesia and the few that exist

are only in the big cities, meaning the people who live in the smaller cities or villages do not have access at all. The bookstores that do exist are small and have limited resources for Bible studies, especially for women. Our hope and prayer is that the study books will be printed and available for women to have in Indonesia so they can have the books they need to study God's Word.

I also sent one book to a missionary friend in Papua. She told me that she read the introduction from the Indonesian "You're Forgiven" book and God reminded her how much He loves her unconditionally and that she has been forgiven. God also reminded her that she also has to love her daughters like that. She continue using the book to dig deeper into God's Word to grow in her faith as a mom, a wife, and a missionary.

Another friend shared with me her story of how she used the printed copy of the Indonesian "David" Bible study book. She made copies of the print outs and brought them to the village where she serve with the local people. They used the study books to do their morning devotional every day before they started their village ministry!

Please be praying for the needs in Indonesia, that these Bible study books will be available for the women not only in the cities, but also in the smaller towns as well. Pray also that God will bring more and more women who are thirsty and hungry for His words. Pray for the people God will bring into Love God Greatly Ministry to partner together as they bring the Gospel to these women, that God will change their lives with the power of His Word, and to equip them to be the salt and light in their families and communities.

THANK YOU SO MUCH for all of your prayers and support of the Love God Greatly Ministry. God is so good and faithful. Praise God!

To connect with LGG Indonesian Branch:

- cintatuhansesungguhnya.wordpress.com
- facebook.com/LGGIndonesia
- instagram/lggindonesia
- twitter.com/lggindonesia
- cintatuhansesungguhnya@gmail.com

Do you know someone who could use our *Love God Greatly* Bible studies in Indonesian? If so, make sure and tell them about LGG Indonesia and all the amazing Bible study resources we provide to help equip them with God's Word!!!

FEAR & ANXIETY

Learning to Overcome with God's Truth

Let's Begin

INTRODUCTION
FEAR & ANXIETY: LEARNING TO OVERCOME
WITH GOD'S TRUTH

Can you imagine life without fear or worry? I can't. It is so much a part of our lives that imagining a life without the smallest fear, worry, or anxiety is pretty much impossible. Adam and Eve were the only ones who were able to experience this kind of life — that is until they disobeyed the perfect law of God. From that moment on, fear and all of its relatives made their home in our hearts.

No one is immune. We all experience it, from mild uneasiness and worry, to crippling anxiety and stark terror. We could spend weeks talking about all the things that rob us of our sleep and torment our minds. Instead of focusing on "what" affects us, we want to look at fear and worry in light of who God is and how we can overcome through the power of Scripture.

But what is fear?
Fear is defined in many different ways. It is a feeling of anxiety or dread concerning the outcome of something. Or the stress of wondering if your needs or desires will be met.

Any number of things can cause fear. It can be ignited through people, circumstances, experiences, hardship, illness, death, loss, pain, the recollection of the past, the unknown of the future, or the stirrings of our imaginations.

Desponding people can find reason for fear where there is no fear; a certain class of persons are greatly gifted with the mournful faculty of inventing troubles; if the Lord has not sent them any trial, they make one for themselves! They have a little trouble-factory in their houses, and they sit down and use their imaginations to meditate terror; - Spurgeon

Fear and anxiety not only affect us mentally, they also affect us physically. Fear puts a knot in your stomach and causes your heart to race. It can make it hard to concentrate or sit still. Fear can cause loss of appetite, or overindulgence, not being able to sleep and weepiness. It feels terrible to be afraid, so it makes perfect sense that we would want to learn how not to be afraid, and how to overcome worry. But there is a deeper and darker level to fear.

Fear is a lack of trust in God. When we let worry take over, we are disobeying God by believing something other than what He has said in His Word. Our fears show unbelief in what God is capable of doing, unbelief in His goodness and care for us, and unbelief in his greatness.

But here is the good news. While we will be exploring some of the things that cause fear, we will also look at how we can overcome our fears through the power of His Word. Our victory will begin when we start looking at who God is and placing our faith in Him and what He has promised to do for His people.

We don't have to be controlled by our fears, and when our eyes are opened to the incredible extent Jesus went to save us — not only from the penalty of sin but also from its power — we will see how fear and anxiety have no foothold in the Christian life.

fear not, for I am with you;
be not dismayed, for I am your God;
Isaiah 41:10

Friend, there is only One who can conquer your circumstances, fears, and anxieties. The one true God who is real and lives. He acts and saves on your behalf because He loves you. He is **your** God.

READING PLAN

WEEK 1
WHAT WE FEAR

MONDAY - Fear of the Future
READ: Jeremiah 29:11, Revelation 1:17-18, Romans 8:28
SOAP: Jeremiah 29:11

TUESDAY - Fear of Disaster
READ: Proverbs 1:33, Proverbs 3:25-26, Luke 6:46-49
SOAP: Proverbs 1:33

WEDNESDAY - Fear of Man
READ: Proverbs 29:25, Isaiah 51:7
SOAP: Proverbs 29:25

THURSDAY - Fear of Loneliness
READ: Isaiah 41:10, Psalm 68:5
SOAP: Isaiah 41:10

FRIDAY - Fear of Not Being in Control
READ: Luke 12:22-26, John 16:33
SOAP: Luke 12:22

WEEK 2
WHY IT'S DANGEROUS TO LIVE IN FEAR & WHAT WE MUST REMEMBER

MONDAY - Shows Lack of Faith
READ: Luke 8:22-25, Mark 4:40
SOAP: Luke 8:25

TUESDAY - It's Unhealthy
READ: Psalm 55:4-5, Psalm 94:19
SOAP: Psalm 94:19

WEDNESDAY - We Are in a War
READ: Isaiah 54:17, 1 Peter 5:8-9, John 10:10
SOAP: Isaiah 54:17

THURSDAY - Condemnation
READ: Romans 8:1-4
SOAP: Romans 8:1

FRIDAY - Fear of the Lord
READ: Proverbs 3:7-8, Proverbs 9:10, Proverbs 14:26-27,
Proverbs 15:33, Proverbs 31:30, Psalm 34:11-14
SOAP: Proverbs 3:7-8

WEEK 3

WHY WE DON'T NEED TO FEAR & WORRY

MONDAY - God is in Control
READ: John 10:27-29, Luke 12:22-31
SOAP: John 10:29

TUESDAY - God Has Delivered Us
READ: Colossians 1:13-14, Psalm 91:1-16
SOAP: Colossians 1:13-14

WEDNESDAY - God Loves Us
READ: Romans 8:31-39, Zephaniah 3:17, 1 John 4:18-19
SOAP: Romans 8:37-39

THURSDAY - God is Powerful
READ: Matthew 28:18, Job 26:7-14
SOAP: Matthew 28:18

FRIDAY - God is Our Strength
READ: Psalm 27:1, 3
SOAP: Psalm 27:1

WEEK 4

WHAT WE MUST BELIEVE AND THINK

MONDAY - Bring Every Thought Captive and Renew Our Minds
READ: 2 Corinthians 10:3-5, Romans 12:2
SOAP: 2 Corinthians 10:5

TUESDAY - Focus Our Mind on the Good
READ: Colossians 3:2, 2 Timothy 1:7, Mark 5:35-43,
Philippians 4:8, Job 3:25, Psalms 23:6, Romans 8:5-7
SOAP: Colossians 3:2

WEDNESDAY - God Will Never Leave
READ: Deuteronomy 31:6, Psalm 23:4
SOAP: Deuteronomy 31:6

THURSDAY - God is Your Help
READ: Psalm 118:5-7, John 17:9-19, Psalm 34:4
SOAP: Psalm 118:5-7

FRIDAY - God is Your Redeemer
READ: Isaiah 41:13-14, Isaiah 43:1-2
SOAP: Isaiah 43:1-2

WEEK 5

WHAT WE MUST SAY

MONDAY - Words of Praise & Worship
READ: Philippians 4:4-7, 1 Thessalonians 5:16, Acts 16:25-26
SOAP: Philippians 4:4

TUESDAY - Words that Declare His Promises
READ: Philippians 4:19, Isaiah 40:29-31, Hebrews 10:19-23
SOAP: Philippians 4:19

WEDNESDAY - Words of Gratitude
READ: Colossians 3:17, 1 Thessalonians 5:18, Psalm 69:30
SOAP: Colossians 3:17

THURSDAY - Words of Prayer
READ: Philippians 4:6-7, 1 Thessalonians 5:17
SOAP: Philippians 4:6

FRIDAY - Words that Build Up
READ: Proverbs 15:4, Ephesians 4:25-32, Matthew 15:11
SOAP: Proverbs 15:4

WEEK 6

WHAT WE MUST DO

MONDAY - Read God's Word and Put on the Armor of God
READ: Ephesians 6:10-18, Psalm 119:105
SOAP: Ephesians 6:11-12

TUESDAY - Commit Everything You Do to the Lord
READ: Proverbs 16:3
SOAP: Proverbs 16:3

WEDNESDAY - Overcome Evil
READ: Romans 12:21
SOAP: Romans 12:21

THURSDAY - Be a Doer of the Word
READ: James 1:22-25, Philippians 4:9
SOAP: James 1:22-23

FRIDAY - Trust God and Do Not fear
READ: Proverbs 3:5-8, Romans 16:20
SOAP: Proverbs 3:5-8

YOUR GOALS

We believe it's important to write out goals for this study. Take some time now and write three goals you would like to focus on as you begin to rise each day and dig into God's Word. Make sure and refer back to these goals throughout the next weeks to help you stay focused. You can do it!

1. Focus my mind & heart to God In the face of fears & anxiety & let His Word be the calm rock I need.

2. Understand that no one is free from worry, but my worries can be lifted up to God.

3. Trust that God won't give me anything I can't handle

Signature: Carleen D Deeg

Date: 05/28/2018

WEEK 1

What We Fear

---

fear not, for I am with you; be not dismayed, for I am your God; I will strengthen you, I will help you, I will uphold you with my righteous right hand.

IS. 41:10

PRAYER

Prayer focus for this week:
Spend time praying for your family members.

MONDAY

TUESDAY

WEDNESDAY

THURSDAY

FRIDAY

CHALLENGE

You can find this listed in our Monday blog post.

MONDAY
Scripture for Week 1

Jeremiah 29:11

11 For I know the plans I have for you, declares the Lord, plans for welfare and not for evil, to give you a future and a hope.

Revelation 1:17-18

17 When I saw him, I fell at his feet as though dead. But he laid his right hand on me, saying, "Fear not, I am the first and the last, 18 and the living one. I died, and behold I am alive forevermore, and I have the keys of Death and Hades."

Romans 8:28

28 And we know that for those who love God all things work together for good, for those who are called according to his purpose.

MONDAY

READ:
Jeremiah 29:11, Revelation 1:17-18, Romans 8:28

SOAP:
Jeremiah 29:11

Scripture

WRITE
OUT THE
SCRIPTURE
PASSAGE
FOR THE
DAY.

For I know the plans I have for you, declares the Lord, plans for welfare & not for evil, to give you a future & a hope

Observations

WRITE
DOWN 1 OR 2
OBSERVATIONS
FROM THE
PASSAGE.

· the Lord has planned out our future well in advance.

· I can have hope of a future

Applications

WRITE DOWN 1 OR 2 APPLICATIONS FROM THE PASSAGE.

- Understand that I have a future planned out for me.

- Nothing will ever be too much for my God to handle.

Pray

WRITE OUT A PRAYER OVER WHAT YOU LEARNED FROM TODAY'S PASSAGE.

Lord, please help me to believe in the plan you have for me & give me the strength to continue down your righteous path for me

Amen.

TUESDAY

Scripture for Week 1

Proverbs 1:33

33 but whoever listens to me will dwell secure
and will be at ease, without dread of disaster.

Proverbs 3:25-26

25 Do not be afraid of sudden terror
or of the ruin of the wicked, when it comes,

26 for the Lord will be your confidence
and will keep your foot from being caught.

Luke 6:46-49

46 "Why do you call me 'Lord, Lord,' and not do what
I tell you? 47 Everyone who comes to me and hears my
words and does them, I will show you what he is like:48 he
is like a man building a house, who dug deep and laid the
foundation on the rock. And when a flood arose, the stream
broke against that house and could not shake it, because
it had been well built. 49 But the one who hears and does
not do them is like a man who built a house on the ground
without a foundation. When the stream broke against it,
immediately it fell, and the ruin of that house was great."

TUESDAY

READ:
Proverbs 1:33, Proverbs 3:25-26, Luke 6:46-49

SOAP:
Proverbs 1:33

Scripture

WRITE
OUT THE
SCRIPTURE
PASSAGE
FOR THE
DAY.

"But whoever listens to me will dwell
secure I will be at ease, without dread
of disaster"

~ Proverbs 1:33

Observations

WRITE
DOWN 1 OR 2
OBSERVATIONS
FROM THE
PASSAGE.

· We are at peace in the Lord's watchful
eye.

· Worry & fear is unnecessary if you
trust in the Lord.

31

Applications

WRITE
DOWN 1 OR 2
APPLICATIONS
FROM THE
PASSAGE.

- I know my worries & years to You

- I will never have to worry when I am
  in the Lord

Pray

WRITE OUT
A PRAYER
OVER WHAT
YOU LEARNED
FROM TODAY'S
PASSAGE.

Lord, help me to release my years & live
in You,

Amen.

WEDNESDAY
Scripture for Week 1

Proverbs 29:25

25 The fear of man lays a snare,
   but whoever trusts in the Lord is safe.

Isaiah 51:7

7 Listen to me, you who know righteousness,
   the people in whose heart is my law;
fear not the reproach of man,
   nor be dismayed at their revilings.

WEDNESDAY

READ:
Proverbs 29:25, Isaiah 51:7

SOAP:
Proverbs 29:25

Scripture

WRITE
OUT THE
SCRIPTURE
PASSAGE
FOR THE
DAY.

"The fear of man lays a snare, but
whoever trusts in the Lord is safe."

~ Proverbs 29:25

Observations

WRITE
DOWN 1 OR 2
OBSERVATIONS
FROM THE
PASSAGE.

· Fear traps us in it

· The Lord is safety.

Applications

WRITE
DOWN 1 OR 2
APPLICATIONS
FROM THE
PASSAGE.

Pray

WRITE OUT
A PRAYER
OVER WHAT
YOU LEARNED
FROM TODAY'S
PASSAGE.

THURSDAY
Scripture for Week 1

Isaiah 41:10
10 fear not, for I am with you;
   be not dismayed, for I am your God;
I will strengthen you, I will help you,
   I will uphold you with my righteous right hand.

Psalm 68:5
5 Father of the fatherless and protector of widows
   is God in his holy habitation.

THURSDAY

READ:
Isaiah 41:10, Psalm 68:5

SOAP:
Isaiah 41:10

Scripture

WRITE
OUT THE
SCRIPTURE
PASSAGE
FOR THE
DAY.

Observations

WRITE
DOWN 1 OR 2
OBSERVATIONS
FROM THE
PASSAGE.

Applications

WRITE
DOWN 1 OR 2
APPLICATIONS
FROM THE
PASSAGE.

Pray

WRITE OUT
A PRAYER
OVER WHAT
YOU LEARNED
FROM TODAY'S
PASSAGE.

FRIDAY
Scripture for Week 1

Luke 12:22-26
22 And he said to his disciples, "Therefore I tell you, do not be anxious about your life, what you will eat, nor about your body, what you will put on. 23 For life is more than food, and the body more than clothing. 24 Consider the ravens: they neither sow nor reap, they have neither storehouse nor barn, and yet God feeds them. Of how much more value are you than the birds! 25 And which of you by being anxious can add a single hour to his span of life? 26 If then you are not able to do as small a thing as that, why are you anxious about the rest?

John 16:33
33 I have said these things to you, that in me you may have peace. In the world you will have tribulation. But take heart; I have overcome the world."

FRIDAY

READ:
Luke 12:22-26, John 16:33

SOAP:
Luke 12:22

Scripture

WRITE
OUT THE
SCRIPTURE
PASSAGE
FOR THE
DAY.

Observations

WRITE
DOWN 1 OR 2
OBSERVATIONS
FROM THE
PASSAGE.

Applications

WRITE
DOWN 1 OR 2
APPLICATIONS
FROM THE
PASSAGE.

Pray

WRITE OUT
A PRAYER
OVER WHAT
YOU LEARNED
FROM TODAY'S
PASSAGE.

REFLECTION QUESTIONS

1. What aspects of the future can make you fearful? Why should we not worry about tomorrow?

2. Scary things happen every day. What truths do we need to preach to ourselves to help us not be fearful?

3. In what ways do we fear man more than God? Why is this dangerous?

4. Why can loneliness be scary? How can we draw comfort from God's omnipresence?

5. We all strive to be in control of our lives. How can that give birth to anxiety? Why does God tell us to be anxious about nothing?

NOTES

WEEK 2

Why It's Dangerous to Live in Fear & What We Must Remember

Be not wise in your own eyes;

fear the LORD,

and turn away from evil.

PROVERBS 3:7

PRAYER

Prayer focus for this week:
Spend time praying for your country.

MONDAY

TUESDAY

WEDNESDAY

THURSDAY

FRIDAY

CHALLENGE

You can find this listed in our Monday blog post.

46

MONDAY
Scripture for Week 2

Luke 8:22-25

22 One day he got into a boat with his disciples, and he said to them, "Let us go across to the other side of the lake." So they set out, 23 and as they sailed he fell asleep. And a windstorm came down on the lake, and they were filling with water and were in danger. 24 And they went and woke him, saying, "Master, Master, we are perishing!" And he awoke and rebuked the wind and the raging waves, and they ceased, and there was a calm. 25 He said to them, "Where is your faith?" And they were afraid, and they marveled, saying to one another, "Who then is this, that he commands even winds and water, and they obey him?"

Mark 4:40

40 He said to them, "Why are you so afraid? Have you still no faith?"

MONDAY

READ:
Luke 8:22-25, Mark 4:40

SOAP:
Luke 8:25

Scripture

WRITE
OUT THE
SCRIPTURE
PASSAGE
FOR THE
DAY.

Observations

WRITE
DOWN 1 OR 2
OBSERVATIONS
FROM THE
PASSAGE.

Applications

WRITE
DOWN 1 OR 2
APPLICATIONS
FROM THE
PASSAGE.

Pray

WRITE OUT
A PRAYER
OVER WHAT
YOU LEARNED
FROM TODAY'S
PASSAGE.

TUESDAY
Scripture for Week 2

Psalm 55:4-5

4 My heart is in anguish within me;
   the terrors of death have fallen upon me.

5 Fear and trembling come upon me,
   and horror overwhelms me.

Psalm 94:19

19 When the cares of my heart are many,
   your consolations cheer my soul.

TUESDAY

READ:
Psalm 55:4-5, Psalm 94:19

SOAP:
Psalm 94:19

Scripture

WRITE
OUT THE
SCRIPTURE
PASSAGE
FOR THE
DAY.

Observations

WRITE
DOWN 1 OR 2
OBSERVATIONS
FROM THE
PASSAGE.

Applications

WRITE
DOWN 1 OR 2
APPLICATIONS
FROM THE
PASSAGE.

Pray

WRITE OUT
A PRAYER
OVER WHAT
YOU LEARNED
FROM TODAY'S
PASSAGE.

WEDNESDAY
Scripture for Week 2

Isaiah 54:17
17 no weapon that is fashioned against you shall succeed,
and you shall refute every tongue that rises against you in judgment.

This is the heritage of the servants of the Lord
and their vindication from me, declares the Lord."

1 Peter 5:8-9
8 Be sober-minded; be watchful. Your adversary the
devil prowls around like a roaring lion, seeking someone to
devour. 9 Resist him, firm in your faith, knowing that the
same kinds of suffering are being experienced by your
brotherhood throughout the world.

John 10:10
10 The thief comes only to steal and kill and destroy. I came
that they may have life and have it abundantly.

WEDNESDAY

READ:
Isaiah 54:17, 1 Peter 5:8-9, John 10:10

SOAP:
Isaiah 54:17

Scripture

WRITE
OUT THE
SCRIPTURE
PASSAGE
FOR THE
DAY.

Observations

WRITE
DOWN 1 OR 2
OBSERVATIONS
FROM THE
PASSAGE.

Applications

WRITE
DOWN 1 OR 2
APPLICATIONS
FROM THE
PASSAGE.

Pray

WRITE OUT
A PRAYER
OVER WHAT
YOU LEARNED
FROM TODAY'S
PASSAGE.

THURSDAY
Scripture for Week 2

Romans 8:1-4

1 There is therefore now no condemnation for those
who are in Christ Jesus. 2 For the law of the Spirit of
life has set you free in Christ Jesus from the law of sin
and death. 3 For God has done what the law, weakened
by the flesh, could not do. By sending his own Son in the
likeness of sinful flesh and for sin, he condemned sin in the
flesh, 4 in order that the righteous requirement of the law
might be fulfilled in us, who walk not according to the flesh
but according to the Spirit.

THURSDAY

READ:
Romans 8:1-4

SOAP:
Romans 8:1

Scripture

WRITE
OUT THE
SCRIPTURE
PASSAGE
FOR THE
DAY.

Observations

WRITE
DOWN 1 OR 2
OBSERVATIONS
FROM THE
PASSAGE.

Applications

WRITE
DOWN 1 OR 2
APPLICATIONS
FROM THE
PASSAGE.

Pray

WRITE OUT
A PRAYER
OVER WHAT
YOU LEARNED
FROM TODAY'S
PASSAGE.

FRIDAY

Scripture for Week 2

Proverbs 3:7-8

7 Be not wise in your own eyes;
    fear the Lord, and turn away from evil.

8 It will be healing to your flesh
    and refreshment to your bones.

Proverbs 9:10

10 The fear of the Lord is the beginning of wisdom,
    and the knowledge of the Holy One is insight.

Proverbs 14:26-27

26 In the fear of the Lord one has strong confidence,
    and his children will have a refuge.

27 The fear of the Lord is a fountain of life,
    that one may turn away from the snares of death.

Proverbs 15:33

33 The fear of the Lord is instruction in wisdom,
    and humility comes before honor.

Proverbs 31:30

30 Charm is deceitful, and beauty is vain,
    but a woman who fears the Lord is to be praised.

Psalm 34:11-14

11 Come, O children, listen to me;
    I will teach you the fear of the Lord.

12 What man is there who desires life
    and loves many days, that he may see good?

13 Keep your tongue from evil
    and your lips from speaking deceit.

14 Turn away from evil and do good;
    seek peace and pursue it.

FRIDAY

READ:
*Proverbs 3:7-8, Proverbs 9:10, Proverbs 14:26-27,
Proverbs 15:33, Proverbs 31:30, Psalm 34:11-14*

SOAP:
Proverbs 3:7-8

Scripture

WRITE
OUT THE
SCRIPTURE
PASSAGE
FOR THE
DAY.

Observations

WRITE
DOWN 1 OR 2
OBSERVATIONS
FROM THE
PASSAGE.

Applications

WRITE
DOWN 1 OR 2
APPLICATIONS
FROM THE
PASSAGE.

Pray

WRITE OUT
A PRAYER
OVER WHAT
YOU LEARNED
FROM TODAY'S
PASSAGE.

REFLECTION QUESTIONS

1. Why are fear and worry a danger to our faith?

2. In what specific ways is worry unhealthy to our bodies?

3. We are always at war against fear. Where do we tend to look for help? Where should we look for help?

4. Why is there no condemnation for those who are in Jesus? How should this affect our worries?

5. What does it mean to fear the Lord? How do we learn to fear Him properly?

NOTES

WEEK 3

Why We Don't Need to Fear & Worry

But in all these things we overwhelmingly conquer through Him who loved us. For I am convinced that neither death, nor life, nor angels, nor principalities, nor things present, nor things to come, nor powers, nor height, nor depth, nor any other created thing, will be able to separate us from the love of God, which is in Christ Jesus our Lord.

ROMANS 8:37-39

PRAYER

WRITE DOWN YOUR PRAYER REQUESTS
AND PRAISES FOR EACH DAY.

Prayer focus for this week:
Spend time praying for your friends.

MONDAY

TUESDAY

WEDNESDAY

THURSDAY

FRIDAY

CHALLENGE

You can find this listed in our Monday blog post.

MONDAY
Scripture for Week 3

John 10:27-29

27 My sheep hear my voice, and I know them, and they
follow me. 28 I give them eternal life, and they will never
perish, and no one will snatch them out of my hand. 29 My
Father, who has given them to me, is greater than all, and no
one is able to snatch them out of the Father's hand.

Luke 12:22-31

22 And he said to his disciples, "Therefore I tell you, do
not be anxious about your life, what you will eat, nor
about your body, what you will put on. 23 For life is more
than food, and the body more than clothing. 24 Consider
the ravens: they neither sow nor reap, they have neither
storehouse nor barn, and yet God feeds them. Of how
much more value are you than the birds! 25 And which of
you by being anxious can add a single hour to his span of
life? 26 If then you are not able to do as small a thing as
that, why are you anxious about the rest? 27 Consider the
lilies, how they grow: they neither toil nor spin, yet I tell
you, even Solomon in all his glory was not arrayed like one
of these. 28 But if God so clothes the grass, which is alive in
the field today, and tomorrow is thrown into the oven, how
much more will he clothe you, O you of little faith! 29 And
do not seek what you are to eat and what you are to drink,
nor be worried. 30 For all the nations of the world seek
after these things, and your Father knows that you need
them. 31 Instead, seek his kingdom, and these things will be
added to you.

MONDAY

READ:
John 10:27-29, Luke 12:22-31

SOAP:
John 10:29

Scripture

WRITE
OUT THE
SCRIPTURE
PASSAGE
FOR THE
DAY.

Observations

WRITE
DOWN 1 OR 2
OBSERVATIONS
FROM THE
PASSAGE.

Applications

WRITE
DOWN 1 OR 2
APPLICATIONS
FROM THE
PASSAGE.

Pray

WRITE OUT
A PRAYER
OVER WHAT
YOU LEARNED
FROM TODAY'S
PASSAGE.

TUESDAY

Scripture for Week 3

Colossians 1:13-14

13 He has delivered us from the domain of darkness and transferred us to the kingdom of his beloved Son, 14 in whom we have redemption, the forgiveness of sins.

Psalm 91:1-16

1 He who dwells in the shelter of the Most High
    will abide in the shadow of the Almighty.

2 I will say to the Lord, "My refuge and my fortress,
    my God, in whom I trust."

3 For he will deliver you from the snare of the fowler
    and from the deadly pestilence.

4 He will cover you with his pinions,
    and under his wings you will find refuge;
    his faithfulness is a shield and buckler.

5 You will not fear the terror of the night,
    nor the arrow that flies by day,

6 nor the pestilence that stalks in darkness,
    nor the destruction that wastes at noonday.

7 A thousand may fall at your side,
    ten thousand at your right hand,
    but it will not come near you.

8 You will only look with your eyes
    and see the recompense of the wicked.

9 Because you have made the Lord your dwelling place—
    the Most High, who is my refuge—

10 no evil shall be allowed to befall you,
    no plague come near your tent.

11 For he will command his angels concerning you
    to guard you in all your ways.

12 On their hands they will bear you up,
    lest you strike your foot against a stone.

13 You will tread on the lion and the adder;
    the young lion and the serpent you will trample underfoot.

14 "Because he holds fast to me in love, I will deliver him;
    I will protect him, because he knows my name.

15 When he calls to me, I will answer him;
    I will be with him in trouble;
    I will rescue him and honor him.

16 With long life I will satisfy him
    and show him my salvation."

TUESDAY

READ:
Colossians 1:13-14, Psalm 91:1-16

SOAP:
Colossians 1:13-14

Scripture

WRITE
OUT THE
SCRIPTURE
PASSAGE
FOR THE
DAY.

Observations

WRITE
DOWN 1 OR 2
OBSERVATIONS
FROM THE
PASSAGE.

Applications

WRITE
DOWN 1 OR 2
APPLICATIONS
FROM THE
PASSAGE.

Pray

WRITE OUT
A PRAYER
OVER WHAT
YOU LEARNED
FROM TODAY'S
PASSAGE.

WEDNESDAY
Scripture for Week 3

Romans 8:31-39

31 What then shall we say to these things? If God is for us, who can be against us? 32 He who did not spare his own Son but gave him up for us all, how will he not also with him graciously give us all things? 33 Who shall bring any charge against God's elect? It is God who justifies. 34 Who is to condemn? Christ Jesus is the one who died—more than that, who was raised—who is at the right hand of God, who indeed is interceding for us. 35 Who shall separate us from the love of Christ? Shall tribulation, or distress, or persecution, or famine, or nakedness, or danger, or sword? 36 As it is written,

"For your sake we are being killed all the day long;
   we are regarded as sheep to be slaughtered."

37 No, in all these things we are more than conquerors through him who loved us.38 For I am sure that neither death nor life, nor angels nor rulers, nor things present nor things to come, nor powers, 39 nor height nor depth, nor anything else in all creation, will be able to separate us from the love of God in Christ Jesus our Lord.

Zephaniah 3:17

17 The Lord your God is in your midst,
   a mighty one who will save;
he will rejoice over you with gladness;
   he will quiet you by his love;
he will exult over you with loud singing.

1 John 4:18-19

18 There is no fear in love, but perfect love casts out fear. For fear has to do with punishment, and whoever fears has not been perfected in love. 19 We love because he first loved us.

WEDNESDAY

READ:
Romans 8:31-39, Zephaniah 3:17, 1 John 4:18-19

SOAP:
Romans 8:37-39

Scripture

WRITE
OUT THE
SCRIPTURE
PASSAGE
FOR THE
DAY.

Observations

WRITE
DOWN 1 OR 2
OBSERVATIONS
FROM THE
PASSAGE.

Applications

WRITE
DOWN 1 OR 2
APPLICATIONS
FROM THE
PASSAGE.

Pray

WRITE OUT
A PRAYER
OVER WHAT
YOU LEARNED
FROM TODAY'S
PASSAGE.

THURSDAY
Scripture for Week 3

Matthew 28:18
18 And Jesus came and said to them, "All authority in heaven and on earth has been given to me."

Job 26:7-14
7 He stretches out the north over the void
   and hangs the earth on nothing.

8 He binds up the waters in his thick clouds,
   and the cloud is not split open under them.

9 He covers the face of the full moon
   and spreads over it his cloud.

10 He has inscribed a circle on the face of the waters
   at the boundary between light and darkness.

11 The pillars of heaven tremble
   and are astounded at his rebuke.

12 By his power he stilled the sea;
   by his understanding he shattered Rahab.

13 By his wind the heavens were made fair;
   his hand pierced the fleeing serpent.

14 Behold, these are but the outskirts of his ways,
   and how small a whisper do we hear of him!
   But the thunder of his power who can understand?"

THURSDAY

READ:
Matthew 28:18, Job 26:7-14

SOAP:
Matthew 28:18

Scripture

WRITE
OUT THE
SCRIPTURE
PASSAGE
FOR THE
DAY.

Observations

WRITE
DOWN 1 OR 2
OBSERVATIONS
FROM THE
PASSAGE.

Applications

WRITE
DOWN 1 OR 2
APPLICATIONS
FROM THE
PASSAGE.

Pray

WRITE OUT
A PRAYER
OVER WHAT
YOU LEARNED
FROM TODAY'S
PASSAGE.

FRIDAY

Scripture for Week 3

Psalm 27:1, 3

1 The Lord is my light and my salvation;
   whom shall I fear?

The Lord is the stronghold of my life;
   of whom shall I be afraid?

3 Though an army encamp against me,
   my heart shall not fear;

though war arise against me,
   yet I will be confident.

FRIDAY

READ:
Psalm 27:1, 3

SOAP:
Psalm 27:1

Scripture

WRITE
OUT THE
SCRIPTURE
PASSAGE
FOR THE
DAY.

Observations

WRITE
DOWN 1 OR 2
OBSERVATIONS
FROM THE
PASSAGE.

Applications

WRITE
DOWN 1 OR 2
APPLICATIONS
FROM THE
PASSAGE.

Pray

WRITE OUT
A PRAYER
OVER WHAT
YOU LEARNED
FROM TODAY'S
PASSAGE.

REFLECTION QUESTIONS

1. Look up verses that talk about God being in control. How much control does God have? How should this affect our fears?

2. List all the things God has delivered us from. Why do we doubt that He can also deliver us from our anxieties and fears?

3. How deep is God's love for us? How should God's love drive out our fears?

4. God's power extends to all things. He even says that he gives us His power. What does this mean in our fight against fear?

5. Sometimes we can feel weak, and in those times our worries can increase. How does understanding the strength of God in our lives help us?

NOTES

WEEK 4

What We Must Believe and Think

---

*Be strong and courageous.
Do not fear or be in dread of
them, for it is the LORD your
God who goes with you. He will
not leave you or forsake you."*

DEUT 31:6

PRAYER

WRITE DOWN YOUR PRAYER REQUESTS
AND PRAISES FOR EACH DAY.

Prayer focus for this week:
Spend time praying for your church.

MONDAY

TUESDAY

WEDNESDAY

THURSDAY

FRIDAY

CHALLENGE

You can find this listed in our Monday blog post.

MONDAY
Scripture for Week 4

2 Corinthians 10:3-5
3 For though we walk in the flesh, we are not waging war
according to the flesh.4 For the weapons of our warfare
are not of the flesh but have divine power to destroy
strongholds. 5 We destroy arguments and every lofty opinion
raised against the knowledge of God, and take every thought
captive to obey Christ.

Romans 12:2
2 Do not be conformed to this world, but be transformed
by the renewal of your mind, that by testing you may discern
what is the will of God, what is good and acceptable and
perfect.

MONDAY

READ:
2 Corinthians 10:3-5, Romans 12:2

SOAP:
2 Corinthians 10:5

Scripture

WRITE
OUT THE
SCRIPTURE
PASSAGE
FOR THE
DAY.

Observations

WRITE
DOWN 1 OR 2
OBSERVATIONS
FROM THE
PASSAGE.

Applications

WRITE
DOWN 1 OR 2
APPLICATIONS
FROM THE
PASSAGE.

Pray

WRITE OUT
A PRAYER
OVER WHAT
YOU LEARNED
FROM TODAY'S
PASSAGE.

TUESDAY

Scripture for Week 4

Colossians 3:2
2 Set your minds on things that are above, not on things that are on earth.

2 Timothy 1:7
7 for God gave us a spirit not of fear but of power and love and self-control.

Mark 5:35-43
35 While he was still speaking, there came from the ruler's house some who said, "Your daughter is dead. Why trouble the Teacher any further?" 36 But overhearing what they said, Jesus said to the ruler of the synagogue, "Do not fear, only believe." 37 And he allowed no one to follow him except Peter and James and John the brother of James. 38 They came to the house of the ruler of the synagogue, and Jesus saw a commotion, people weeping and wailing loudly.39 And when he had entered, he said to them, "Why are you making a commotion and weeping? The child is not dead but sleeping." 40 And they laughed at him. But he put them all outside and took the child's father and mother and those who were with him and went in where the child was. 41 Taking her by the hand he said to her, "Talitha cumi," which means, "Little girl, I say to you, arise." 42 And immediately the girl got up and began walking (for she was twelve years of age), and they were immediately overcome with amazement. 43 And he strictly charged them that no one should know this, and told them to give her something to eat.

Philippians 4:8
8 Finally, brothers, whatever is true, whatever is honorable, whatever is just, whatever is pure, whatever is lovely, whatever is commendable, if there is any excellence, if there is anything worthy of praise, think about these things.

Job 3:25
25 For the thing that I fear comes upon me,
    and what I dread befalls me.

Psalms 23:6
6 Surely goodness and mercy shall follow me
    all the days of my life,
and I shall dwell in the house of the Lord forever.

Romans 8:5-7
5 For those who live according to the flesh set their minds on the things of the flesh, but those who live according to the Spirit set their minds on the things of the Spirit. 6 For to set the mind on the flesh is death, but to set the mind on the Spirit is life and peace. 7 For the mind that is set on the flesh is hostile to God, for it does not submit to God's law; indeed, it cannot.

TUESDAY

READ:
*Colossians 3:2, 2 Timothy 1:7, Mark 5:35-43,
Philippians 4:8, Job 3:25, Psalms 23:6, Romans 8:5-7*

SOAP:
Colossians 3:2

Scripture

WRITE
OUT THE
SCRIPTURE
PASSAGE
FOR THE
DAY.

Observations

WRITE
DOWN 1 OR 2
OBSERVATIONS
FROM THE
PASSAGE.

Applications

WRITE
DOWN 1 OR 2
APPLICATIONS
FROM THE
PASSAGE.

Pray

WRITE OUT
A PRAYER
OVER WHAT
YOU LEARNED
FROM TODAY'S
PASSAGE.

WEDNESDAY
Scripture for Week 4

Deuteronomy 31:6

6 Be strong and courageous. Do not fear or be in dread of them, for it is the Lordyour God who goes with you. He will not leave you or forsake you.

Psalm 23:4

4 Even though I walk through the valley of the shadow of death,

    I will fear no evil,
for you are with me;
    your rod and your staff,
    they comfort me.

WEDNESDAY

READ:
Deuteronomy 31:6, Psalm 23:4

SOAP:
Deuteronomy 31:6

Scripture

WRITE
OUT THE
SCRIPTURE
PASSAGE
FOR THE
DAY.

Observations

WRITE
DOWN 1 OR 2
OBSERVATIONS
FROM THE
PASSAGE.

Applications

WRITE
DOWN 1 OR 2
APPLICATIONS
FROM THE
PASSAGE.

Pray

WRITE OUT
A PRAYER
OVER WHAT
YOU LEARNED
FROM TODAY'S
PASSAGE.

THURSDAY
Scripture for Week 4

Psalm 118:5-7

5 Out of my distress I called on the Lord;
   the Lord answered me and set me free.

6 The Lord is on my side; I will not fear.
   What can man do to me?

7 The Lord is on my side as my helper;
   I shall look in triumph on those who hate me.

John 17:9-19

9 I am praying for them. I am not praying for the world but for those whom you have given me, for they are yours. 10 All mine are yours, and yours are mine, and I am glorified in them. 11 And I am no longer in the world, but they are in the world, and I am coming to you. Holy Father, keep them in your name, which you have given me, that they may be one, even as we are one. 12 While I was with them, I kept them in your name, which you have given me. I have guarded them, and not one of them has been lost except the son of destruction, that the Scripture might be fulfilled. 13 But now I am coming to you, and these things I speak in the world, that they may have my joy fulfilled in themselves. 14 I have given them your word, and the world has hated them because they are not of the world, just as I am not of the world. 15 I do not ask that you take them out of the world, but that you keep them from the evil one. 16 They are not of the world, just as I am not of the world. 17 Sanctify them in the truth; your word is truth. 18 As you sent me into the world, so I have sent them into the world. 19 And for their sake I consecrate myself, that they also may be sanctified in truth.

Psalm 34:4

4 I sought the Lord, and he answered me
   and delivered me from all my fears.

THURSDAY

READ:
Psalm 118:5-7, John 17:9-19, Psalm 34:4

SOAP:
Psalm 118:5-7

Scripture

WRITE
OUT THE
SCRIPTURE
PASSAGE
FOR THE
DAY.

Observations

WRITE
DOWN 1 OR 2
OBSERVATIONS
FROM THE
PASSAGE.

Applications

WRITE
DOWN 1 OR 2
APPLICATIONS
FROM THE
PASSAGE.

Pray

WRITE OUT
A PRAYER
OVER WHAT
YOU LEARNED
FROM TODAY'S
PASSAGE.

FRIDAY

Scripture for Week 4

Isaiah 41:13-14

13 For I, the Lord your God,
   hold your right hand;
it is I who say to you, "Fear not,
   I am the one who helps you."

14 Fear not, you worm Jacob,
   you men of Israel!
I am the one who helps you, declares the Lord;
   your Redeemer is the Holy One of Israel.

Isaiah 43:1-2

1 But now thus says the Lord,
he who created you, O Jacob,
   he who formed you, O Israel:
"Fear not, for I have redeemed you;
   I have called you by name, you are mine.

2 When you pass through the waters, I will be with you;
   and through the rivers, they shall not overwhelm you;
when you walk through fire you shall not be burned,
   and the flame shall not consume you.

FRIDAY

READ:
Isaiah 41:13-14, Isaiah 43:1-2

SOAP:
Isaiah 43:1-2

Scripture

WRITE
OUT THE
SCRIPTURE
PASSAGE
FOR THE
DAY.

Observations

WRITE
DOWN 1 OR 2
OBSERVATIONS
FROM THE
PASSAGE.

Applications

WRITE DOWN 1 OR 2 APPLICATIONS FROM THE PASSAGE.

Pray

WRITE OUT A PRAYER OVER WHAT YOU LEARNED FROM TODAY'S PASSAGE.

REFLECTION
QUESTIONS

1. What does it mean to take every thought captive? How do we do this?

2. What are some things we should set our minds on instead?

3. God promised never to leave us. What does He mean by this?

4. List all the ways that God is our help.

5. Jesus is your Redeemer. You belong to Him. How can this truth help you kill your fears?

NOTES

WEEK 5

What We Must Say

Be anxious for nothing, but
in everything by prayer and
supplication with thanksgiving let
your requests be made known to
God. And the peace of God, which
surpasses all comprehension, will
guard your hearts and your minds
in Christ Jesus.

PHIL 4:6-7

PRAYER

WRITE DOWN YOUR PRAYER REQUESTS
AND PRAISES FOR EACH DAY.

Prayer focus for this week:
Spend time praying for missionaries.

MONDAY

TUESDAY

WEDNESDAY

THURSDAY

FRIDAY

CHALLENGE

You can find this listed in our Monday blog post.

MONDAY

Scripture for Week 5

Philippians 4:4-7

4 Rejoice in the Lord always; again I will say, rejoice. 5 Let
your reasonableness be known to everyone. The Lord
is at hand; 6 do not be anxious about anything, but in
everything by prayer and supplication with thanksgiving
let your requests be made known to God. 7 And the peace
of God, which surpasses all understanding, will guard your
hearts and your minds in Christ Jesus.

1 Thessalonians 5:16

16 Rejoice always.

Acts 16:25-26

25 About midnight Paul and Silas were praying and
singing hymns to God, and the prisoners were listening
to them, 26 and suddenly there was a great earthquake,
so that the foundations of the prison were shaken. And
immediately all the doors were opened, and everyone's bonds
were unfastened.

MONDAY

READ:
READ:
Philippians 4:4-7, 1 Thessalonians 5:16, Acts 16:25-26

SOAP:
Philippians 4:4

Scripture

WRITE
OUT THE
SCRIPTURE
PASSAGE
FOR THE
DAY.

Observations

WRITE
DOWN 1 OR 2
OBSERVATIONS
FROM THE
PASSAGE.

Applications

WRITE
DOWN 1 OR 2
APPLICATIONS
FROM THE
PASSAGE.

Pray

WRITE OUT
A PRAYER
OVER WHAT
YOU LEARNED
FROM TODAY'S
PASSAGE.

TUESDAY
Scripture for Week 5

Philippians 4:19
19 And my God will supply every need of yours according to his riches in glory in Christ Jesus.

Isaiah 40:29-31
29 He gives power to the faint,
  and to him who has no might he increases strength.

30 Even youths shall faint and be weary,
  and young men shall fall exhausted;

31 but they who wait for the Lord shall renew their strength;
  they shall mount up with wings like eagles;

they shall run and not be weary;
  they shall walk and not faint.

Hebrews 10:19-23
19 Therefore, brothers, since we have confidence to enter the holy places by the blood of Jesus, 20 by the new and living way that he opened for us through the curtain, that is, through his flesh, 21 and since we have a great priest over the house of God, 22 let us draw near with a true heart in full assurance of faith, with our hearts sprinkled clean from an evil conscience and our bodies washed with pure water. 23 Let us hold fast the confession of our hope without wavering, for he who promised is faithful.

TUESDAY

READ:
Philippians 4:19, Isaiah 40:29-31, Hebrews 10:19-23

SOAP:
Philippians 4:19

Scripture

WRITE
OUT THE
SCRIPTURE
PASSAGE
FOR THE
DAY.

Observations

WRITE
DOWN 1 OR 2
OBSERVATIONS
FROM THE
PASSAGE.

Applications

WRITE
DOWN 1 OR 2
APPLICATIONS
FROM THE
PASSAGE.

Pray

WRITE OUT
A PRAYER
OVER WHAT
YOU LEARNED
FROM TODAY'S
PASSAGE.

WEDNESDAY
Scripture for Week 5

Colossians 3:17

17 And whatever you do, in word or deed, do everything in the name of the Lord Jesus, giving thanks to God the Father through him.

1 Thessalonians 5:18

18 give thanks in all circumstances; for this is the will of God in Christ Jesus for you.

Psalm 69:30

30 I will praise the name of God with a song;
   I will magnify him with thanksgiving.

WEDNESDAY

READ:
Colossians 3:17, 1 Thessalonians 5:18, Psalm 69:30

SOAP:
Colossians 3:17

Scripture

WRITE
OUT THE
SCRIPTURE
PASSAGE
FOR THE
DAY.

Observations

WRITE
DOWN 1 OR 2
OBSERVATIONS
FROM THE
PASSAGE.

Applications

WRITE
DOWN 1 OR 2
APPLICATIONS
FROM THE
PASSAGE.

Pray

WRITE OUT
A PRAYER
OVER WHAT
YOU LEARNED
FROM TODAY'S
PASSAGE.

THURSDAY

Scripture for Week 5

Philippians 4:6-7

6 do not be anxious about anything, but in everything by prayer and supplication with thanksgiving let your requests be made known to God. 7 And the peace of God, which surpasses all understanding, will guard your hearts and your minds in Christ Jesus.

1 Thessalonians 5:17

17 pray without ceasing.

THURSDAY

READ:
Philippians 4:6-7, 1 Thessalonians 5:17

SOAP:
Philippians 4:6

Scripture

WRITE
OUT THE
SCRIPTURE
PASSAGE
FOR THE
DAY.

Observations

WRITE
DOWN 1 OR 2
OBSERVATIONS
FROM THE
PASSAGE.

Applications

WRITE
DOWN 1 OR 2
APPLICATIONS
FROM THE
PASSAGE.

Pray

WRITE OUT
A PRAYER
OVER WHAT
YOU LEARNED
FROM TODAY'S
PASSAGE.

FRIDAY

Scripture for Week 5

Proverbs 15:4

4 A gentle tongue is a tree of life,
  but perverseness in it breaks the spirit.

Ephesians 4:25-32

25 Therefore, having put away falsehood, let each one of
you speak the truth with his neighbor, for we are members
one of another. 26 Be angry and do not sin; do not let the
sun go down on your anger, 27 and give no opportunity to
the devil.28 Let the thief no longer steal, but rather let him
labor, doing honest work with his own hands, so that he
may have something to share with anyone in need. 29 Let
no corrupting talk come out of your mouths, but only such
as is good for building up, as fits the occasion, that it may
give grace to those who hear. 30 And do not grieve the
Holy Spirit of God, by whom you were sealed for the day
of redemption.31 Let all bitterness and wrath and anger and
clamor and slander be put away from you, along with all
malice. 32 Be kind to one another, tenderhearted, forgiving
one another, as God in Christ forgave you.

Matthew 15:11

11 it is not what goes into the mouth that defiles a person,
but what comes out of the mouth; this defiles a person.

FRIDAY

READ:
Proverbs 15:4, Ephesians 4:25-32, Matthew 15:11

SOAP:
Proverbs 15:4

Scripture

WRITE
OUT THE
SCRIPTURE
PASSAGE
FOR THE
DAY.

Observations

WRITE
DOWN 1 OR 2
OBSERVATIONS
FROM THE
PASSAGE.

Applications

WRITE
DOWN 1 OR 2
APPLICATIONS
FROM THE
PASSAGE.

Pray

WRITE OUT
A PRAYER
OVER WHAT
YOU LEARNED
FROM TODAY'S
PASSAGE.

REFLECTION QUESTIONS

1. We should rejoice always, even in the midst of fear and anxiety. Why?

2. How can reminding ourselves of the promises God has made to us help us in moments of fear?

3. In what ways does God supply all of our needs? What if it's not in the way we want or expect?

4. What role does thanksgiving play in overcoming fear?

5. Instead of being anxious we are told to pray. How is this helpful? Write a prayer about something you are fearful or anxious about. Hold nothing back.

NOTES

WEEK 6
What We Must Do

Commit your work to the LORD, and your plans will be established.

PROVERBS 16:3

PRAYER

Prayer focus for this week:
Spend time praying for you.

MONDAY

TUESDAY

WEDNESDAY

THURSDAY

FRIDAY

CHALLENGE

You can find this listed in our Monday blog post.

MONDAY
Scripture for Week 6

Ephesians 6:10-18

10 Finally, be strong in the Lord and in the strength of his might. 11 Put on the whole armor of God, that you may be able to stand against the schemes of the devil. 12 For we do not wrestle against flesh and blood, but against the rulers, against the authorities, against the cosmic powers over this present darkness, against the spiritual forces of evil in the heavenly places. 13 Therefore take up the whole armor of God, that you may be able to withstand in the evil day, and having done all, to stand firm. 14 Stand therefore, having fastened on the belt of truth, and having put on the breastplate of righteousness, 15 and, as shoes for your feet, having put on the readiness given by the gospel of peace. 16 In all circumstances take up the shield of faith, with which you can extinguish all the flaming darts of the evil one; 17 and take the helmet of salvation, and the sword of the Spirit, which is the word of God, 18 praying at all times in the Spirit, with all prayer and supplication. To that end, keep alert with all perseverance, making supplication for all the saints.

Psalm 119:105

105 Your word is a lamp to my feet
   and a light to my path.

MONDAY

READ:
Ephesians 6:10-18, Psalm 119:105

SOAP:
Ephesians 6:11-12

Scripture

WRITE
OUT THE
SCRIPTURE
PASSAGE
FOR THE
DAY.

Observations

WRITE
DOWN 1 OR 2
OBSERVATIONS
FROM THE
PASSAGE.

Applications

WRITE
DOWN 1 OR 2
APPLICATIONS
FROM THE
PASSAGE.

Pray

WRITE OUT
A PRAYER
OVER WHAT
YOU LEARNED
FROM TODAY'S
PASSAGE.

TUESDAY
Scripture for Week 6

Proverbs 16:3
3 Commit your work to the Lord,
   and your plans will be established.

TUESDAY

READ:
Proverbs 16:3

SOAP:
Proverbs 16:3

Scripture

WRITE
OUT THE
SCRIPTURE
PASSAGE
FOR THE
DAY.

Observations

WRITE
DOWN 1 OR 2
OBSERVATIONS
FROM THE
PASSAGE.

Applications

WRITE
DOWN 1 OR 2
APPLICATIONS
FROM THE
PASSAGE.

Pray

WRITE OUT
A PRAYER
OVER WHAT
YOU LEARNED
FROM TODAY'S
PASSAGE.

WEDNESDAY
Scripture for Week 6

Romans 12:21
21 Do not be overcome by evil, but overcome evil with good.

WEDNESDAY

READ:
Romans 12:21

SOAP:
Romans 12:21

Scripture

WRITE
OUT THE
SCRIPTURE
PASSAGE
FOR THE
DAY.

Observations

WRITE
DOWN 1 OR 2
OBSERVATIONS
FROM THE
PASSAGE.

Applications

WRITE
DOWN 1 OR 2
APPLICATIONS
FROM THE
PASSAGE.

Pray

WRITE OUT
A PRAYER
OVER WHAT
YOU LEARNED
FROM TODAY'S
PASSAGE.

THURSDAY

Scripture for Week 6

James 1:22-25

22 But be doers of the word, and not hearers only, deceiving yourselves. 23 For if anyone is a hearer of the word and not a doer, he is like a man who looks intently at his natural face in a mirror. 24 For he looks at himself and goes away and at once forgets what he was like. 25 But the one who looks into the perfect law, the law of liberty, and perseveres, being no hearer who forgets but a doer who acts, he will be blessed in his doing.

Philippians 4:9

9 What you have learned and received and heard and seen in me—practice these things, and the God of peace will be with you.

THURSDAY

READ:
James 1:22-25, Philippians 4:9

SOAP:
James 1:22-23

Scripture

WRITE
OUT THE
SCRIPTURE
PASSAGE
FOR THE
DAY.

Observations

WRITE
DOWN 1 OR 2
OBSERVATIONS
FROM THE
PASSAGE.

Applications

WRITE
DOWN 1 OR 2
APPLICATIONS
FROM THE
PASSAGE.

Pray

WRITE OUT
A PRAYER
OVER WHAT
YOU LEARNED
FROM TODAY'S
PASSAGE.

FRIDAY

Scripture for Week 6

Proverbs 3:5-8

5 Trust in the Lord with all your heart,
   and do not lean on your own understanding.

6 In all your ways acknowledge him,
   and he will make straight your paths.

7 Be not wise in your own eyes;
   fear the Lord, and turn away from evil.

8 It will be healing to your flesh
   and refreshment to your bones.

Romans 16:20

20 The God of peace will soon crush Satan under your
feet. The grace of our Lord Jesus Christ be with you.

FRIDAY

READ:
Proverbs 3:5-8, Romans 16:20

SOAP:
Proverbs 3:5-8

Scripture

WRITE
OUT THE
SCRIPTURE
PASSAGE
FOR THE
DAY.

Observations

WRITE
DOWN 1 OR 2
OBSERVATIONS
FROM THE
PASSAGE.

Applications

WRITE
DOWN 1 OR 2
APPLICATIONS
FROM THE
PASSAGE.

Pray

WRITE OUT
A PRAYER
OVER WHAT
YOU LEARNED
FROM TODAY'S
PASSAGE.

REFLECTION
QUESTIONS

1. In Ephesians 6 we are told to put on the armor of God because we are soldiers fighting against sin and evil. How do the different parts of the armor help us fight fear and worry?

2. What does it mean to commit your plans to the Lord?

3. Give some examples of how we can overcome evil with good. How can we also overcome fear with good?

4. It is easy to read and talk about all the things we should be doing, but James reminds us that we must be doers of the Word. Why is this important?

5. Ultimately fear is banished when we trust God. How can we grow in our faith, and how does strong faith kill sin?

NOTES

KNOW THESE TRUTHS
from God's Word

God loves you.

Even when you're feeling unworthy and like the world is stacked against you, God loves you - yes, you - and He has created you for great purpose.

God's Word says, "God so loved the world that He gave His one and only Son, Jesus, that whoever believes in Him shall not perish, but have eternal life" (John 3:16).

Our sin separates us from God.

We are all sinners by nature and by choice, and because of this we are separated from God, who is holy.

God's Word says, "All have sinned and fall short of the glory of God" (Romans 3:23).

Jesus died so that you might have life.

The consequence of sin is death, but your story doesn't have to end there! God's free gift of salvation is available to us because Jesus took the penalty for our sin when He died on the cross.

God's Word says, "For the wages of sin is death, but the free gift of God is eternal life in Christ Jesus our Lord" (Romans 6:23); "God demonstrates His own love toward us, in that while we were yet sinners, Christ died for us" (Romans 5:8).

Jesus lives!

Death could not hold Him, and three days after His body was placed in the tomb Jesus rose again, defeating sin and death forever! He lives today in heaven and is preparing a place in eternity for all who believe in Him.

God's Word says, "In my Father's house are many rooms. If it were not so, would I have told you that I go to prepare a place for you? And if I go and prepare a place for you, I will come again and will take you to myself, that where I am you may be also" (John 14:2-3).

Yes, you can KNOW that you are forgiven.
Accept Jesus as the only way to salvation...

Accepting Jesus as your Savior is not about what you can do, but rather about
having faith in what Jesus has already done. It takes recognizing that you are
a sinner, believing that Jesus died for your sins, and asking for forgiveness by
placing your full trust in Jesus's work on the cross on your behalf.

God's Word says, "If you confess with your mouth that Jesus is Lord and believe
in your heart that God raised him from the dead, you will be saved. For with the
heart one believes and is justified, and with the mouth one confesses and is saved"
(Romans 10:9-10).

Practically, what does that look like?
With a sincere heart, you can pray a simple prayer like this:

God,
I know that I am a sinner.
I don't want to live another day without embracing
the love and forgiveness that You have for me.
I ask for Your forgiveness.
I believe that You died for my sins and rose from the dead.
I surrender all that I am and ask You to be Lord of my life.
Help me to turn from my sin and follow You.
Teach me what it means to walk in freedom as I live under Your grace,
and help me to grow in Your ways as I seek to know You more.
Amen.

If you just prayed this prayer (or something similar in your own words), would
you email us at info@lovegodgreatly.com?

We'd love to help get you started on this exciting journey as a child of God!

WELCOME FRIEND

We're so glad you're here

Love God Greatly exists to inspire, encourage, and equip women all over the world to make God's Word a priority in their lives.

INSPIRE
women to make God's Word a priority in their daily lives through our Bible study resources.

ENCOURAGE
women in their daily walks with God through online community and personal accountability.

EQUIP
women to grow in their faith, so that they can effectively reach others for Christ.

Love God Greatly consists of a beautiful community of women who use a variety of technology platforms to keep each other accountable in God's Word.

We start with a simple Bible reading plan, but it doesn't stop there.

Some gather in homes and churches locally, while others connect online with women across the globe. Whatever the method, we lovingly lock arms and unite for this purpose...to Love God Greatly with our lives.

At Love God Greatly, you'll find real, authentic women. Women who are imperfect, yet forgiven. Women who desire less of us, and a whole lot more of Jesus. Women who long to know God through his Word, because we know that Truth transforms and sets us free. Women who are better together, saturated in God's Word and in community with one another.

Love God Greatly is a 501 (C) (3) non-profit organization. Funding for Love God Greatly comes through donations and proceeds from our online Bible study journals and books. LGG is committed to providing quality Bible study materials and believes finances should never get in the way of a woman being able to participate in one of our studies. All journals and translated journals are available to download for free from LoveGodGreatly.com for those who cannot afford to purchase them. Our journals and books are also available for sale on Amazon. Search for "Love God Greatly" to see all of our Bible study journals and books. 100% of proceeds go directly back into supporting Love God Greatly and helping us inspire, encourage and equip women all over the world with God's Word.

THANK YOU for partnering with us!

WHAT WE OFFER:

18 + Translations | Bible Reading Plans | Online Bible Study
Love God Greatly App | 80 + Countries Served
Bible Study Journals & Books | Community Groups

EACH LGG STUDY INCLUDES:

Three Devotional Corresponding Blog Posts
Memory Verses | Weekly Challenge | Weekly Reading Plan
Reflection Questions And More!

OTHER LOVE GOD GREATLY STUDIES INCLUDE:

David | Ecclesiastes | Growing Through Prayer | Names Of God
Galatians | Psalm 119 | 1st & 2nd Peter | Made For Community | Esther
The Road To Christmas | The Source Of Gratitude | You Are Loved

Visit us online at
LOVEGODGREATLY.COM